ANGEL CATCHER

A JOURNAL OF LOSS AND REMEMBRANCE

by Kathy Eldon and Amy Eldon Turteltaub

CHRONICLE BOOKS

SAN FRANCISCO

© 2008 Kathleen M. Eldon
Illustrations © 2008 Susy Pilgrim-Waters

ISBN 978-0-8118-6172-4
Design by Michael Morris
Illustrations by Susy Pilgrim-Waters/Lilla Rogers Studio
Typeset in HTF Requiem and Gotham
Manufactured in China

Chronicle Books endeavors to use environmentally responsible paper in its gift and stationery products.

10 9 8 7 6

Chronicle Books LLC
680 Second Street
San Francisco, CA 94107
www.chroniclebooks.com

Visit www.creativevisions.org to find out more about the work of Kathy Eldon and Amy Eldon Turteltaub.

DEDICATION

for Dan, our inspiration, and for Michael Bedner and Jon Turteltaub, with
whom we have found great joy and peace.

WHAT IS AN ANGEL CATCHER?

Amy and I have created this book based on our own experience in surviving the most profound loss we could ever imagine—the murder of my son, Dan, a talented young Reuters photographer, who was stoned to death by an angry mob in Somalia on July 12, 1993. Dan was 22 when he was killed. Amy had just turned 18.

In the days, weeks, and months after Dan's death, I felt pain I cannot now begin to describe. I learned lessons I never wanted to learn and discovered parts of me I was not aware existed. Sometimes I raged. Often I wept. At times I did not even wish to live.

Early on, I bought books on grieving, hoping that by reading about the process, I might hurry myself through the pain. But I found it almost impossible to read, much less comprehend, books with so many words on a page, and soon I abandoned the attempt. Since Dan's death, I have read many volumes about the process of mourning, and I have learned there are certain stages we must go through if we are to fully recover from the loss of a loved one.

An initial feeling of disbelief and shock is almost universal. Certainly I was numb for several weeks after the devastating phone call informing me of my son's death. I couldn't really feel anything and viewed the world as though through a hazy mist. At first I was insulated from my feelings by the urgency of all I had to do: There was a memorial service to plan, friends to contact, and many decisions to be made. Soon, however, the numbness and shock began to alternate with a denial of what had happened. I didn't want to believe the truth. My mind played tricks on me, and I saw Dan everywhere: darting off trains and buses, mingling with crowds, disappearing around corners. When the phone rang, I absurdly hoped that it was my son calling. Eventually I wanted to escape, to sleep, to dream him alive again.

After that, I got angry. I cursed my fate and raged against life itself. There were times when I literally tore at the curtains and walls of my home, traumatized by the truth I could no longer deny. It was then that I frightened myself with the tears that came in waves, like breakers on a desolate shore.

Out of my rage was born a deep sense of guilt. Was I in some way responsible for what had happened? Was there something I could have done? Over time I made myself sick with worry, wondering how Dan's death could have been avoided. My release came through pouring my energy into projects for young people, which helped transform my guilt and anger into something with which I could live.

Eventually, I slowly began to accept Dan's death. But strangely enough, this was the hardest time of all. The idea of forgetting Dan, even for an hour at a time, felt like a betrayal of my son. Worse still, I found that my vivid memories of our life together were beginning to blur; his characteristic gestures and outrageous wit were not as clear as they had been; the stories I loved to tell were fading from my memory.

I couldn't remember incidents we had shared, moments I had always thought were indelibly etched in my mind.

Amy was going through her own time of despair. She and Dan had been unusually close, and she felt as though a part of her had been amputated when he died. Two years after Dan's death, she called me from college. "I can't remember everything about him!" she sobbed. "I'm forgetting so much. I'm scared I won't remember anything one day!"

Desperately searching for something to soothe her, I happened to catch sight of a dreamcatcher hanging over my bed. Created by Native American craftsmen to "capture" bad dreams, the little bentwood hoop, decorated with feathers and beads, triggered something in my mind.

"I know," I said "We'll make an angel catcher."

"What's that?" she said.

"It's a book to capture an angel," I said logically. "You can fill it with pictures, stories, letters, whatever will remind you of Dan. You'll have something to keep forever. One day you can show it to your children when they ask you about their uncle."

There was a moment of silence, and then Amy began to speak, excitedly describing all the things she wanted to include in her book.

Two months later, she came home for a visit and pulled a black bound book from her suitcase. "It's my angel catcher," she said proudly. Together we turned the pages of her journal. I laughed, then cried at my daughter's rendering of her brother's memory. With words, pictures, drawings, and quotations, Amy had captured the essence of Dan's spirit. Every page brought back a world of memories, reminding me of who Dan was—and who he still is in the minds of those who love him.

Amy and I showed the angel catcher to friends who had suffered the loss of someone dear to them and discovered that many people wanted to use the ideas to create their own book. At first we photocopied the pages, but soon we couldn't keep up with the demand!

Our Angel Catcher is designed to help you capture the essence of a person who is no longer with you—to preserve forever the memories of the time you shared together. Its empty pages become yours to fill with words, pictures, drawings, and poems—even recipes, quotations, and songs.

But the Angel Catcher is more than that. By creating your own special journal, you can fully experience your feelings about the person you have lost, and in so doing, move through the sadness of loss to calm acceptance, and ultimately a new, greater sense of joy and fulfillment.

We wish you a gentle journey.

Kathy Eldon

At first, after my brother died, I wanted to hang on to everything that he had ever owned or touched. One day, I found a dusty old back-pack in Dan's room. Rummaging through it, I discovered an ancient toothbrush buried under a pile of photographs and papers. I wanted to treasure it forever. I eventually forced myself to throw away the toothbrush and his battered comb because I realized that the person who had made them special to me is with me always—through my memories. For a long time, I pulled out those memories, one at a time, and used them to crawl back into the past. It gave me comfort to recall details of our lives together and helped me feel less lonely. But one horrible day, I realized my memories were fading. It was then that my mother suggested that I make an angel catcher for Dan.

Creating a journal of remembrance is a very personal and private thing. There are no rules for how to use it. The pages don't need to be filled in any particular order, nor do you have to fill in every entry. Go through it at your own pace, bringing to it your own unique experiences.

The words on each page are designed to trigger your thoughts and feelings. Sometimes they may be negative, for even if we love some-one, we don't always like everything about them! Put it all down. No matter how much energy it takes, force yourself to go deep inside and dig for the buried memories. You can always tear up the pages, cover them with pictures, or paste a sheet of paper over them if you don't want anyone to see what you have written. Sometimes you may feel like screaming and throwing the book against the wall—that's okay, too. Expressing yourself freely—no holds barred—will be the key to recovering the memories of your loved one while restoring your sense of peace.

This is your angel catcher. Use it as your companion on the long journey through the deep sadness of loss into the great joy which comes with recovery. And as you fill the pages of this book, think about your own life. Do you have any regrets? Are you being true to yourself? Are you leading the life of your choice? Reflect on those people you love, who will one day perhaps create a journal for you. Are you letting them know how you feel? Most importantly, are you creating the kind of memories you wish to leave behind? If not, now's the time to begin.

Amy Eldon Turteltaub

I FEEL AFRAID

SLOW MOTION

Everything I do today is in slow motion.
I feel numb.
My mind doesn't work.
I can't make decisions.
Here is what I absolutely must do

I'M VERY TIRED

I'm very tired now.
I know I need to rest because my emotions are taking over.
I'll feel better if I

YOU SAID / I SAID

This was our last conversation

This is the last conversation I want to remember

SLEEPLESS

When I can't sleep, I am thinking about

I know you would say

Next time I can't sleep I am going to

Watching you go was

I wanted to say

I wanted you to say

At the time I felt

Now I feel

WHEN I HEARD

When I heard you were gone, I

I felt

I FEEL ALONE

My mind is so full of worries I sometimes think I must be going crazy. Here's what I need help to get through

THE MEMORIAL SERVICE

The funeral/memorial service was today.

The most important thing about it for me was

SYMPATHY CARDS, GIFTS, AND LETTERS

Letters received

Letters acknowledged

....

....

....

....

....

....

....

....

....

....

....

....

....

....

....

....

....

....

....

....

Letters received

Letters acknowledged

....

....

....

....

....

....

....

....

....

....

....

....

....

....

....

....

....

....

....

....

DATE

Dear

I miss you.
I miss the way you

I miss the way we

I miss being with you when we

It will help me feel better if I

I visited your grave today.
I felt

TRUST

I am finding it hard to trust anyone right now . . . especially myself.
You would say

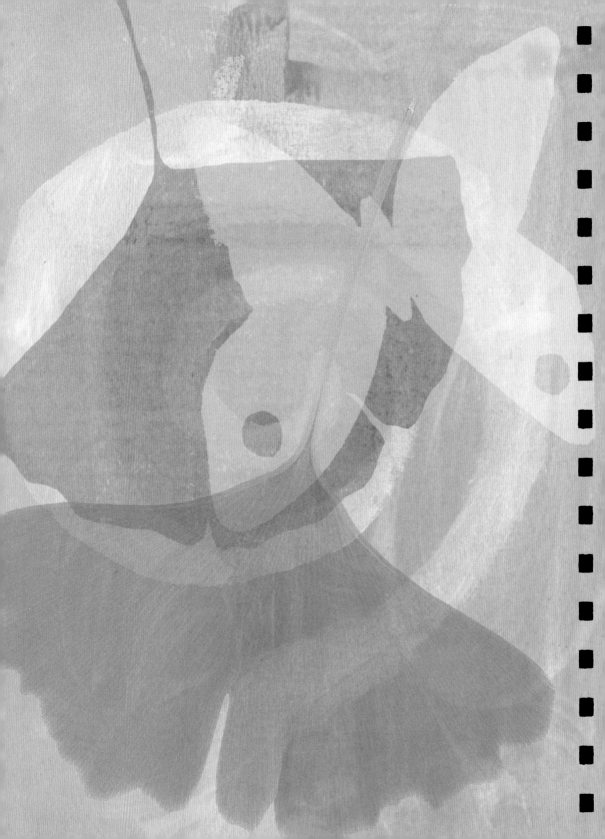

REMEMBERING

This is a .... day for me.
I am remembering where I was when I heard the news.
The first thing I did was

The hardest thing for me today is

Here's how my head feels

My heart feels

Here's what I am going to do to remember you today

SICK INSIDE

The sadness makes me physically ill sometimes. I feel

It goes away when

I worry that

Sometimes the pain is so great I

To make me feel better I am going to

GUILT

I can't seem to stop feeling guilty.

Here's what I am feeling

Here's what you would say to me

ROLLER COASTER

Lately, I feel like I'm on a roller coaster. My emotions are all over the place. Here's where I am on the ride

I believe one day I'll be safe again, back on solid ground.

FRUSTRATIONS

Some days I get so frustrated I want to scream, punch pillows, and break things. I never knew I had the capacity to get so angry. Looking back, I can hardly believe what I did.

The only person I want to talk to about my feelings is you.
You would say

MISERABLE TODAY

Why bother getting out of bed in the morning? I don't want to see anyone. I don't want to do anything.

I feel

I know I must

To get through this day I will

HIDING

I want to hide away from the world. I don't like going out. I feel like I'll scare people away. No one knows how to be with me right now. I keep thinking they expect me to break down and cry.

You would say

I made it through another day. I hated nearly every minute, but I did it. Tomorrow is another day. I am not looking forward to it, either, but somehow I will get through. I can't wait till I don't feel this way anymore. I want to be excited about my days.

Here's what you would say to me

CELEBRATION

I get angry when I see people in the world who are still alive, when you aren't! But then I remember I must celebrate the people who are still around me. I must make sure I have no unfinished business with anyone. Life is too short to be little.

I must call

I must write

I must visit

I must touch

I LOVE YOU

I love you.

I love the way you

I love the way we

I loved it when we

I will always remember how you

It's hard for me to be without you when I

Here's what I am going to do to show my love for you

WHERE ARE YOU NOW?

I wonder where you are now. I think you are

SURRENDER

I surrender.
When I let go, I feel

I keep wondering how you would have been if I had died first. What sort of funeral would you have given me?

What would you have said about me?

How would you be now?

SPECIAL

It's hard for me to deal with the things you left behind.
I want to keep track of who has what.

As a memento, I would like to save

1.

2.

3.

4.

5.

6.

7.

8.

TREASURES

And give away

1.

2.

3.

4.

5.

6.

7.

8.

SCREAMING DAYS

Some days I feel like screaming. Today is one of them. It's because

When you were upset, you used to

When I am done screaming, I am going to

MEAN THOUGHTS

I am really angry at you for leaving me.

When something exciting happens, you are the first person I want to tell. Here's what has just happened

This is what you would say to me

I FEEL YOU

I keep wishing you would give me a sign to show me you are around sometimes.

I think you are near when

SPECIAL TREATS

I miss our special treats.
Today I'll treat myself.
You would have wanted me to

DREAMING OF YOU

I would like to dream about you.

In my dream, we would

I would say

You would say

SAYINGS

I remember what you used to say to me

And what you used to say to

I find myself saying

Here's what I know you would say to me now

SONGS

Your favorite song was

We used to sing

When you sang I felt

Here are some of your other favorite songs

SWALLOWING MY MEMORIES

I remember what fun we used to have when we went out for a meal together. You used to love

Sometimes it seems very hard to want to be happy now that we can't go out together. Right now I would like to

I loved when you cooked

Recipe for:

Ingredients

Preparation:

Recipe for:

Ingredients

Preparation:

When I eat .... I think of you.

When I drink .... I remember you.

I remember my favorite meal with you

I am going to remember you by

I feel sad today. I know one quick way to feel better is to help someone else.

Today I will

I remember how you used to

In your memory I want to

Please tell me what else I can do for others

NEW BEGINNINGS

I need to make a statement!

Today I am going to

REDECORATE · CHANGE MY HAIRSTYLE · ADOPT A PET ·
GO TO A CONCERT / MUSEUM / MOVIE / LECTURE
TAKE A CLASS · MAKE A NEW FRIEND

To every thing there is a season, and a time to every purpose
under the heaven:
A time to be born, and a time to die; a time to plant, and a
time to pluck up that which is planted;
A time to kill, and a time to heal; a time to break down, and
a time to build up;
A time to weep, and a time to laugh; a time to mourn, and a
time to dance;
A time to cast away stones, and a time to gather stones
together; a time to embrace, and a time to refrain from
embracing;
A time to get, and a time to lose; a time to keep, and a time
to cast away;
A time to rend, and a time to sew; a time to keep silence,
and a time to speak;
A time to love, and a time to hate; a time of war, and a time
of peace.

Ecclesiastes, 3:1–8

DREAMING ABOUT YOU

I had a dream about you.

In it, you were

I was

When I woke up I felt

I think the dream means

LEARNING TO FLY

When you died, I felt like I had been hit by a plank. I could barely stand up, much less walk. I kept losing my balance and bumping into walls. Right now, I am learning to walk again. One day, I hope I can fly.

Here's where I am right now

JOY

I felt joy today—the first spark of lightness since you died.

I wanted to tell you about it.

PAIN

I'm hurting a lot today. I know I need to do something to get through this pain. I could go for a walk, have a massage, call up a friend, eat something delicious, listen to wonderful music, cook a meal for a friend, create something magical, take a child to a film, talk about you, watch a film we shared, call up your friends, look at old pictures, go to our favorite place, cry a little, cry a lot, pray, feel my courage, and know you are near.

Here's what I am going to do

SECRET THOUGHTS

I know how you felt about me. Sometimes you didn't say it out loud, but I knew what you were thinking.

MIRRORS

The world sees me one way. You used to see me another.
Here's what the outside of my head looks like today

Here's what the inside of my head looks like

Here's how I feel inside my stomach today

Here's what you would tell me to do

PICTURES OF YOU

When I see pictures of you I feel

These are my favorite pictures of you

PICTURES OF ME

You took this picture of me. Afterward we

PICTURES OF US

These are my favorite pictures of us together.

BELLY LAUGHS

I can't keep from laughing when I remember

I loved your face when you

Your laugh was like

You always laughed when I

I always laughed when you

Right now I can imagine you are smiling because

I want to laugh more often. Here's what I will do in your memory

Do not stand at my grave and weep.
I am not there. I do not sleep.
I am a thousand winds that blow;
I am a diamond's glint on snow.
I am the sunlight on ripened grain;
I am the gentle autumn's rain.
When you awaken in the morning's hush,
I am the swift uplifting rush
of quiet birds in circled flight.
I am the soft star that shines at night.
Do not stand at my grave and cry,
I am not there.

I did not die.

Anonymous

VISITING YOU

I visited your favorite place today.

I felt

NO WAY OUT BUT THROUGH

I can't believe people ask me if I have gotten over you.
I never want to.
I do want to get through the pain of losing you.

TREASURES

If I could have anything of yours, here's what I would like to have

Here's why

This is what I would do with it

I don't have it, so I am going to give myself another treasure to remember you.

My treasure will be

HEALING

Some days, I feel like I have a whole new perspective on life. Then little things like a stubbed toe, a parking ticket, or a missed appointment don't seem to matter. On those days, I feel like I can handle anything.

Other days . . .

FEARS

Now that you aren't here anymore, I am frightened of

When you were here, I was afraid of

I remember how you acted when I was afraid

Remembering you helps me not be afraid of

TIRED

I am tired of feeling so much.
I want to stop hurting.
Please help.

Give sorrow words; the grief that does not speak whispers the o'er fraught heart and bids it break.

William Shakespeare

When I knew you had died, I felt

Here's how I am feeling now

Before you died, I wish we had

It upsets me to think that

It makes me mad when I remember

Why did you have to leave me?

LETTER TO GOD

Dear God,

DATE

Today is your birthday. You would have been .... years old.

The month leading up to this day has been particularly hard for me.
I have felt like

Today I feel

On your birthday we used to

Once I gave you

Once you gave me

We used to celebrate by

Today I am going to give myself a present from you. It will be

DATE

Today is my birthday.

Today I feel

On my birthday you always used to

To celebrate my birthday, I will give myself a present from you.

HOLIDAYS

Holidays are hard without you.

Today is

Here's how I am feeling without you today

Today is

Here's how I am feeling without you today

CHRISTMAS / CHANUKAH / RAMADAN

This is the first holiday season I have had to live without you.

Here's how I feel

I remember how you used to

My favorite present from you was

This year I am going to give myself a present from you.
It will be

Here's what I wish I could give you

I remember when you

To make me feel better I am going to

I am going to share this time with

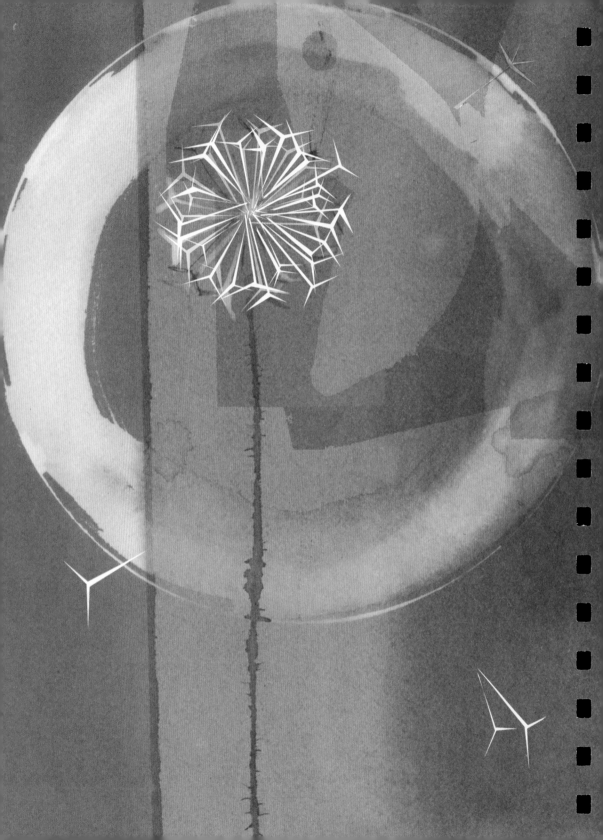

I thought anniversaries were meant to be happy. This one is very sad. I am afraid of the pain I may feel on the anniversary of your death. Here is how I am going to remember you today

Here's who I shall share the day with

Here's what we will do

We will celebrate your life!

LAUGHING

I laughed out loud today at something I knew you'd find funny.

SHARE YOUR LOVE

A sample letter to send to your friends on the anniversary of the passing of your loved one. Fill in the blanks and add your own ideas. Better still, have a gathering of friends and share your love.

On .... , it will be one year since .... passed away. But before you roll over and sleep through the day, think of what .... would have done!

In joyous commemoration of the life of .... do something you have always wanted to do!

CHOOSE FROM THE FOLLOWING OR COME UP WITH YOUR OWN LIST.

Take someone you love on a picnic

Play your favorite music

Plan a vacation day

Give something away

Do something you have always been afraid to do

Sing on the sidewalk

Go dancing

Donate your time to someone you love

Cook your favorite meal

Begin a picture album

PUSHING ME

You always encouraged me to

Now that you aren't here, I have to do it myself. Today I will

I know you would also want me to

I think you would be proud of the fact that I

I am worried that I will forget the special times we shared together. I want to remember them forever.

I never want to forget the way you

I never want to forget how we were together when I

MEMORIES ARE LIKE BUTTERFLIES

I never want to forget how you

I never want to forget

Here's what I would like to forget

I get really angry when I think we will never be able to

Here's what I need to do with other people to make sure that I won't have any more regrets in my life

I get really angry when I think you will never see me

Dear

There are many things I meant to tell you when we were together, but somehow the time didn't seem right. Today, I have the time, and I need to say what I wasn't able to say before.

First, let me say that I am sorry I

Sometimes I felt

I know you felt

I love you.

GOALS

We used to talk about my goals in life. They keep changing.
Here are my latest—and how I think you would feel about them.

I FEEL BRAVE

I felt you near me.

It happened

When I felt you close by, I was

I felt

It would make me .... to feel you close again.

When I see pictures of disasters or accidents on television, or read stories about people who have died in the paper, I understand what each grieving mother, father, son, daughter, grandparent, wife, or child must feel.

I feel connected to their pain in a way I never felt before.

I know how I felt when people reached out to me.

I want to reach out to

DYING

Here's how I'm feeling about death now

Before I die, here's what I want to do!

For what is it to die, but to stand naked in the wind and to melt into the sun?
And what is it to cease breathing, but to free the breath from its restless tides,
that it may rise and expand and seek God unencumbered.
Only when you drink from the river of silence shall you indeed sing.
And when you have reached the mountain top, then you shall begin to climb.
And when the earth shall claim your limbs, then shall you truly dance.

Kahlil Gibran

SOARING

Right after you died, I imagined you

Now I think you are

If I am quiet and listen carefully, I can hear your voice inside me.
Here is what it is saying

Losing you has changed me. Some changes are good, others not so good. Here are some good changes

Here are some not-so-good changes

Here's who I would like to be

Here's how I must change to get there

CELEBRATION

To commemorate and celebrate your life, I want to create something
that will live on.

PLANT A TREE · WRITE A POEM · START A GARDEN
PAINT A PICTURE · HELP A CHILD IN NEED

I WILL NEVER FORGET YOU

You will live in me always.
Your words, your touch, your heart, your soul are all part of me.
My heart is full of your memories.
My spirit has been
forever touched by you.
Thank you for the gift of your life.
I will never forget you.

HELPFUL READINGS

We have found these books helpful in understanding the process of grieving:

BEATTIE, MELODY. *The Grief Club: The Secret to Getting Through All Kinds of Change.* Hazelden, 2006.
Part memoir, part self-help book, part journal, this book will help members of a very special "club"—those who have survived the loss of a child.

D'ARCY, PAULA. *When People Grieve: The Power of Love in the Midst of Pain.* Crossroad Publishing Company, 2005.
A classic manual full of practical advice for dealing with pain, loss, and bereavement.

DEVITA-RAEBURN, ELIZABETH. *The Empty Room: Understanding Sibling Loss.* Scribner, 2007.
The author explores the tools a grieving sibling needs to heal and move forward.

DONNELLY, KATHERINE FAIR. *Recovering from the Loss of a Parent.* iUniverse, 2000.
How to get through the stress arising from the death of a parent.

EDELMAN, HOPE. *Motherless Daughters: The Legacy of Loss.* Da Capo Press, 2006.
Provides understanding and comfort to a woman after the death of her mother.

ELDON, AMY. *Angel Catcher For Kids: A Journal to Help You Remember the Person Who Died.* Chronicle Books, 2002.
Designed to help a child overcome the loss of a loved one.

FELBER, MARTA. *Finding Your Way After Your Spouse Dies.* Ave Maria Press, 2000.
A guide for coping with the practical issues that face the recently widowed.

KUBLER-ROSS, DR. ELISABETH. *On Death and Dying.* Scribner, 1997.
Dr. Kubler-Ross's timeless book explores the five stages of grief and offers a better understanding of how imminent death affects a patient and the patient's family.